T0196620

The Beautiful Art of Poetry

Carol Schroeder

authorHOUSE®

AuthorHouse™
1663 Liberty Drive
Bloomington, IN 47403
www.authorhouse.com
Phone: 833-262-8899

Published by AuthorHouse   03/26/2021

ISBN: 978-1-6655-2133-8 (sc)
ISBN: 978-1-6655-2132-1 (e)

Print information available on the last page.

This book is printed on acid-free paper.

Contents

A Friend Thats Like A Sister

DATE: 3 /8 02

YOU'RE A FRIEND OF MINE
IT'S LIKE A WONDERFUL SIGN
THAT YOU WILL ALWAYS BE APART OF ME
THAT'S THE WAY I WANT IT TO BE
YOU ARE ALWAYS ON MY MIND
BECAUSE YOU'RE SO KIND
ILL ALWAYS TRY TO FIND A WAY
TO MAKE YOUR DAY
EVEN IF IT'S WORDS THAT I SAY
I LOVE YOU
THAT WILL ALWAYS REMAIN TRUE
FOR YOU ARE MY FRIEND
THAT I WILL KEEP TO THE END
YOU'RE LIKE A SISTER TO ME
THAT'S WHAT I SEE
YOU ARE THE ONE THAT HOLDS THE KEY
FOR US TO REMAIN THAT WAY FOREVER
YOU ARE MY FRIEND AND SISTER TOGETHER
YOU KNOW HOW TO LIGHT UP MY DAY
WHEN IM BLUE
YOU ALWAYS KNOW JUST WHAT TO SAY
YOU'RE A FRIEND THAT IS TRUE
I WONT FALL BEHIND
YOU'RE A FRIEND OF MINE.

DATE: 5 16 05

A SPECIAL FRIEND OF MINE
GIVE A WONDERFUL SIGN
THAT WILL ALWAYS BE APART OF ME
THE WAY IT SHOULD BE
YOU'RE SO KIND
THAT'S WHY YOU'RE ALWAYS ON MY MIND
TRYING TO FIND A WAY
TO BRIGHTEN YOUR DAY
EVEN IF I SAY
I LOVE YOU
THAT'S ALWAYS TRUE
YOU'RE A FRIEND
TO THE END
THAT'S LIKE A MOM TO ME
THIS IS WHAT I SEE
A FRIEND THAT WILL NEVER FLEE
THAT WILL REMAIN FOREVER
A FRIEND THAT CAN BE LIKE A MOM
AND FRIEND TOGETHER
YOU LIGHT UP MY DAY
SO I WONT BE BLUE
YOU KNOW JUST WHAT TO SAY
A FRIEND IS TRUE
THAT'S HARD TO FIND
I KNOW I WONT FALL BEHIND
WHEN YOU'RE A FRIEND OF MINE.

Complicated

THIS IS A COMPLICATED WORLD
THIS IS A COMPLICATED LIFE
LOVE IS COMPLICATED
GUYS ARE REALLY COMPLICATED
TRUST IS SO COMPLICATED
THIS IS SUCH A COMPLICATED TIME
THIS IS A COMPLICATED SUBJECT
CARING IS COMPLICATED
FRIENDS ARE SO COMPLICATED
HEARTS ARE VERY COMPLICATED
STRENGTH IS COMPLICATED WHEN YOU HURT
WARMTH IS ALL WE NEED WITH THIS COMPLICATED HEART
WHY DO WE HAVE TO BE SO COMPLICATED
LOVE IS VERY COMPLICATED
TO BE WITH A BROKEN HEART IS MORE COMPLICATED
TO NEED A FRIEND IS COMPLICATED
WHY SHOULD WE MAKE THIS WORLD SO COMPLICATED
WHEN IT CAN BE EASY WITH ALL THINGS
IF YOU JUST TRY TO MAKE IT EASY
IT'S THE EASIEST THING

Eagles

DATE: 12 10 96

EAGLES SO WILD AND FREE
SO RARE AND BEAUTIFUL
THEY FLY SO HIGH
IN THE SKY
YET THEY AREN'T SO FREE
THEY ARE AN ENDANGERED SPECIES
THEY ARE AT RI8K
I WISH I WAS AN EAGLE
TO BE ABLE TO FLY SO HIGH
TO HAVE NO WORRIES
UP THERE IN THAT BEAUTIFUL SKY
EAGLES NEVER LIE
OR GIVE YOU THAT LINE
EAGLES SO RARE
YET SO SCARED
EAGLES SO FREE
BUT NOT ME
EAGLES SO WILD
YET SO MILD
EAGLES SO HIGH IN THE SKY
YET THEY NEVER LIE
I WISH I WAS AN EAGLE
YET I WANT TO STAY WHO I AM.
EAGLES.

AS THE ROCK SHAPES
AS THE ROAD TURNS
AS WE DRIVE THROUGH
THE WINDING ROADS
I THINK OF HOW BEAUTIFUL LIFE IS
AT ESCALANTE CANYON
I WONDER WHAT IS BEHIND
THE ROAD THAT TURNS
AS THE SUN BURNS
I WONDER WHAT'S BEHIND
THE ROCK SHAPES
HOW BEAUTIFUL ALL THIS IS
ESCALANTE CANYON
AS THE MYSTERY BUILDS
AS THE ROADS WIND
AS IT TURNS
AS THE ROCK MAKES SHAPE
AT ESCALANTE CANYON
WILL ALWAYS BE A PLACE
FOR YOU AND ME TO BE ALONE
ESCALANTE CANYON.

UP IN THE MOUNTAINS
WITH ALL THE WATER FALLS
THAT FLOW LIKE FOUTAINS
WERE THERE'S NO WALLS
THAT IS A PLACE TO BE
WERE THE HEART CAN FEEL FREE
WITH EVERYTHING THAT YOU'VE SEEN
YOU'LL KNOW WHAT I MEAN
WHEN YOU LOOK UP IN THE SKY
FROM A PLACE UP HIGH
IN THE MOUNTAINS
WERE THE WATER FLOWS LIKE FOUTAINS
THAT YOU CAN FEEL FREE
THERE'S NO OTHER PLACE TO BE
WERE YOU FEEL AT PEACE
WERE EVERYTHING SEEMS TO SEIZE
AND WHAT YOU FEEL
WILL SEEM SO REAL
EVEN AT NIGHT
EVERYTHING FEELS SO BRIGHT
WHEN YOU'RE IN THE MOUNTAINS.

WHEN I LOSE YOU
WHEN I CARE FOR YOU
WHEN I LOVED YOU
WHEN I THINK ABOUT YOU
IT IS FORGETTING YOU
IS WHAT IS HARD
WHEN YOU LET GO
FORGETTING YOU IS HARD
WHEN YOU'RE OVER ME
FORGETTING YOU IS HARD
WHEN YOU LET YOUR FRIENDS TAKE OVER YOUR LIFE
FORGETTING YOU IS HARD
IT IS HARD FOR ME TO FORGET YOU
WHEN FORGETTING YOU IS HARD TO DO
SO IM NOT GOING TO LET YOU GO
IM NOT GOING TO FORGET YOU
BECAUSE YOU'RE EVERYTHING IN THE WORLD TO ME
I LOVE YOU
I CARE FOR YOU
I THINK OF YOU
IT IS FORGETTING YOU IS WHAT IS HARD TO DO.

DRIFTING THROUGH THIS TOTAL DEPRESSION
IN SEARCH OF SOMETHING TO HOLD ON TO
SOME IDENTITY OF MY LIFE
I WONDER IS ALL OF THIS FOR REAL OR JUST ILLUSION
OF MY LIFE? IS IT TEMPORARY OR FOR INFINITY
I TRAVEL IN FOR A DESTINATION WITHOUT A CLUE
ABOUT MY LIFE SITUATION AHEAD
WHEN WILL I KNOW WHAT MY FUTURE HOLDS
THAT IS UP TO ME WHAT IT SHOULD HOLD
SHOULD I BE WORRIED ABOUT WHAT IT HOLDS FOR ME
OR JUST GO WITH IT
WILL I BE LOVED
WILL I SEE THE ANSWERS SOMEDAY
WILL IT SHOW ME WHAT'S AHEAD
BUT MY FUTURE IS WAITING FOR ME
SOMEWHERE IN TIME
WHEN I GET TO MY FUTURE I WILL WORRY THEN
BUT TILL THEN I WILL JUST WAIT AND LIVE DAY BY DAY
SO I CAN LIVE WITHOUT WORRY
I WILL WAIT FOR MY FUTURE AND HOPE
IT HOLDS GOOD ANSWERS
TO MY QUESTIONS THAT I SEEK

I Have A Heart

DATE: 10 8 98

I HAVE A HEART
THAT WILL GIVE YOU A START
IT'S FULL OF LOVE
FOR THAT SPECIAL DOVE
SO I WONT BE SHY
FOR THAT ILL TRY
WILL I EVER FIND
WHAT I HAVE IN MIND
LOVE CAN MAKE ME BLIND
SO WILL I EVER SEE
WHAT'S IN STORE FOR ME
OR HOLDS THE KEY
ALL I KNOW IS
THAT I HAVE A HEART
FOR THIS
I KNOW I CAN GIVE YOU A PART
OF MY HEART
FOR THIS IS ONLY A START
I WANT THAT DANCE
SO ILL TAKE THAT CHANCE
SO ILL LIVE
WITH WHAT I CAN GIVE
ILL GIVE YOU A PART OF MY HEART
THAT IS A START
I CAN GIVE LOVE
FOR THAT SPECIAL DOVE
I CAN GIVE ALL OF THIS
AND MORE BECAUSE OF MY HEART.

Life

DATE: 12 4 93

LIFE IS SPECIAL
LIFE IS NOT SOMETHING TO TAKE ADVANTAGE OF
YOU ALWAYS HAVE LOVE
YOU MAY HAVE UPS AND DOWNS
EVERYBODY HAS HIS OR HER TROUBLES ONCE IN A WHILE
LOVE IS ALWAYS THERE THROUGH TEARS AND LAUGHTER
THINGS MAY NOT GO YOUR WAY
THINGS WILL GET BETTER SOMEDAY
YOU MAY NOT KNOW WHAT TO DO
IT MAY MAKE YOU BLUE
LIFE CAN BE BRIGHT
WHEN YOU SEE THE LIGHT
THINGS MAY NOT BE RIGHT
THAT MAKES YOU CRY
NOT UNDERSTANDING WHY
WITH EVERYTHING YOU HAVE SEEN
YOU WILL UNDERSTAND WHAT I MEAN
YOU MAY NOT ALWAYS KNOW
WHAT TO DO
BUT LOVE CAN GROW
WHEN SOMEONE LOVES YOU
LIFE IS EASIER
THINGS WILL GET BETTER SOMEDAY
YOU WILL GET YOUR WAY

REMEMBER LIFE WILL ALWAYS BE THERE
AFTER THE TEARS AND THE PAIN
YOU'LL LOSE YOUR FEARS
LOVE WILL GAIN
WHEN YOU SHARE
LIFE WITH SOMEONE
EVERYTHING WILL BE DONE
DON'T LET LIFE GET YOU DOWN
YOU ALWAYS HAVE SOMEONE TO LIFT YOU UP OFF THE GROUND
LIFE.

My Life

DATE: 10 8 92

LIFE IS LIKE A WHIRLWIND
OF COLORS PASSING ME BY
I DON'T KNOW WHY
I WANT TO CRY
I THOUGHT I LOST IT ALL
WHEN MY HEART TOOK A FALL
TILL I FOUND A FRIEND
WHO HELPED ME MEND
WHEN I DIDN'T HAVE THE STRENGTH
HE HELPED ME GO THE LENGTH
I THOUGHT IT WAS OVER
TILL HE GAVE ME A SHOULDER
I THOUGHT I WOULD GROW COLDER
MY LIFE
WAS SO BLACK
BECAUSE OF WHAT I LACKED
TILL HE GAVE ME HIS HAND
LIFTED ME OUT OF THE SAND
HE IS A FRIEND
WHO HELPED ME MEND
I DON'T KNOW WHY
MY LIFE STILL FEELS LIKE A WHIRLWIND
OF COLORS PASSING ME BY
I KNOW ILL TRY
NOT TO CRY
INSTEAD ILL FLY
AND SAY BYE-BYE
TO MY LIFE
THAT CUTS LIKE A KNIFE!
MY LIFE.

Racism

DATE: 3 16 92

IT'S NOT THE COLOR
IT'S NOT THE RELIGION
IT'S NOT THE RACE
WE ARE ALL STILL HUMAN
WE ARE ALL DIFFERENT IN SOME WAY
JUST WITH DIFFERENT THINGS TO SAY
WE ARE ALL STILL EQUAL
THAT WILL ALWAYS MEAN SOMETHING
WE COULD ALWAYS SING
IT'S NOT WHAT COLOR WE ARE
IT'S WHAT WE HAVE ON THE INSIDE
THE TRUE PERSON WE ARE THAT EVERYBODY HIDES
THAT DEFINES US ALL
IT'S WHAT COMES FROM THE HEART
THAT VERY SPECIAL PART
IT'S WHAT'S IN OUR MIND
YOU ARE ALWAYS KIND
OUR FEELINGS ARE STILL THE SAME
NO MATTER FROM WHERE YOU CAME
TO BE HERE
YOU ALWAYS HAVE A FRIEND NEAR.

Race

DATE: 4 2 96

WHAT IS RACE
WHY DO WE HAVE TO FACE THAT
BECAUSE WE ARE DIFFERENT
OR ARE WE UNIQUE
THAT'S WHAT I THINK
IT HURTS WHEN THEY ARE MEAN
BUT I HAVE SEEN
ALL I WANT
EVERYTHING IN THIS WORLD
CAN BE A SONG
BECAUSE THEY DON'T THINK
ABOUT WHAT'S WRONG
SO THEY SINK
BECAUSE THEY DON'T KNOW HOW TO SING
TO WHAT'S RIGHT
SO FOLLOW ON A ANGELS WING
TO THE LIGHT
BECAUSE THERE IS SOMETHING
WE DON'T HAVE TO FACE
THAT' IS RACE

A Friend Like You

DATE: 10 21 00

I'VE NEVER KNOWN A TRUE FRIEND
SOMEONE TO KEEP TO THE END
TILL I MET YOU
WHO IS TRUE
SOMEONE WHO I LOVE
LIKE THEY WERE SENT FROM ABOVE
SOMEONE THAT I THOUGHT I WOULD NEVER FIND
WHO IS SO KIND
TILL I FOUND A FRIEND LIKE YOU
I DON'T KNOW WHY
I ALWAYS WANTED TO CRY
TILL I FOUND A FRIEND LIKE YOU
SOMEONE WHO KNOWS WHEN IM BLUE
THAT NO MATTER WHAT IS ALWAYS TRUE
I KNOW ILL NEVER FIND A FRIEND
LIKE YOU
I FINALLY FOUND A TRUE FRIEND
SOMEONE I CAN KEEP TO THE END
ILL NEVER HAVE TO LOOK AGAIN
FOR YOU ARE MY TRUE FRIEND
ILL NEVER LET YOU GO
FOR YOU ARE MY FRIEND THAT I LOVE
NOW THE LIGHT SHINES BRIGHT
EVEN IN THE DARKEST OF NIGHTS
CAUSE I HAVE
A FRIEND LIKE YOU.

Afraid 2

DATE: 4 2 96

AFRAID TO GO ON
AFRAID TO FACE THE DAWN
I DON'T KNOW WHAT'S WRONG
EXCEPT THAT IM AFRAID
I DON'T KNOW WHY
IM FADING TO WHAT I'VE MADE
THERE'S ALWAYS A SONG
THAT MAKES ME CRY
I DON'T KNOW WHAT TO DO
ILL ALWAYS TRY
EVEN THOUGH THERE'S NOTHING NEW
BECAUSE IM AFRAID
OF WHAT IM GOING TO FACE
SO I WILL ALWAYS CARRY MACE
I KNOW IT COULD BE A BEAUTIFUL DAY
SO MAYBE ILL FIND A WAY
TO GET OUT
EVEN THOUGH I DON'T KNOW WHAT IT'S ALL ABOUT
THERE IS ALWAYS SOMETHING THAT IM AFRAID OF
SO I DON'T LOVE
BECAUSE I CAN'T FIND THAT ONE CERTAIN DOVE
BUT ILL ALWAYS TRY
I DON'T KNOW WHY
I ALWAYS CRY
I GUESS ILL ALWAYS BE AFRAID.

Alone

DATE: 11 2 93

LOVE IS IN THE AIR
LOVE IS IN THE SAND
AS I WALK DOWN THE SANDY BEACH
ALL AONE AS I WALK,
NO ONE IN SIGHT BUT THERE IS LOVE IN THE AIR
I MAY WALK ALONE BUT IM NOT ALONE
WHEN THERE IS LOVE AROUND
AS I WALK ALONE
I KEEP ON WALKING DOWN THE SANDY BEACH
FEELING ALL THE LOVE IN THE AIR
I HAVE A LOT OF LOVE TO SHARE
I WILL ALWAYS CARE
WHEN THERE IS LOVE IN THE AIR
YOU ARE NEVER ALONE
WHEN LOVE IS SHOWN
WHAT A BEAUTIFUL WAY
TO SPEND ON THIS BEAUTIFUL DAY
WALKING DOWN A SANDY BEACH
LOVE WITH IN ARMS REACH
I LOVE TO LOVE YOU
THAT'S THE BEST THING TO DO
YOURE THE BEST THING TO ME
YOURE ALL I SEE
MY HEART FLYS FREE
THE LOVE I HAVE FROM YOU
WILL NEVER MAKE ME BLUE
WITH YOUR LOVE AROUND IM NEVER ALONE.

Can't Let You Go

DATE: 10 27 93

I CANT LET YOU GO
YOU ARE SO MUCH OF MY HEART
YOU ARE THE KEY TO WHAT'S IN MY HEART
YOU ARE A DREAM
YOU HAVE SUCH GOOD QUALITIES
YOU ARE SO TRUE
THAT I CAN NEVER BE BLUE
YOU ARE WHAT I'VE BEEN LOOKING FOR
I COULDN'T ASK FOR MORE
YOU PULLED ME OUT OF THE CLOUDS
YOU ARE ALWAYS THERE FOR ME
YOU SET MY HEART FREE
THAT MY HEART SOARS
LIKE THE WAVES THAT HIT'S THE OCEAN SHORES
YOU ARE MY HEART, MY SOUL, MY FATE
I CANT LET YOU GO
I DON'T HAVE THE STRENGTH
BUT I WILL GO THE LENGTH
MY EYES GLOW
EVERYTIME I LOOK AT YOU
I REALLY LOVE YOU
THAT'S WHY I CAN'T LET YOU GO.

Eagles And Friendship

DATE: 2 25 00

AS THE EAGLE SOARS
MY LOVE SEES ALL
EVERYTHING THAT FALLS
AS THE OCEAN WATER HIT'S THE SHORES
MY HEART HAS MORE
THEN THAT OF THE OCEAN SHORE
AS I SEE THE REDNESS IN THE SKYS
AND EVERYTHING THAT FLYS
THROUGH THAT I FEEL
WHAT IS REAL
AS YOU REACHED OUT YOUR HAND
TO PICK ME UP OUT OF THE SAND
I STILL SEE OUR FRIENDSHIP
THAT WE HAVE
I WAS GLAD
THAT I HAVE YOU
AS A FRIEND
THAT IS TRUE
THE MOUNTAINS IN THE SKY
WHERE THE EAGLES FLY
OUR FRIENDSHIP STILL SEES ALL
EVERYTHING THAT FALLS
OUR FRIENDSHIP STILL LIVES ON,
WHEN WERE NOT STRONG
WE WILL ALWAYS HAVE A SHOULDER TO LEAN ON
WE STILL HAVE EACH OTHER
WITH OUR FRIENDSHIP TOGETHER
IT WILL ALWAYS BE STRONG
JUST LIKE THE EAGLE WHO SOARS
WHO SEES IT ALL
OUR FRIENDSHIP TOGETHER WILL NEVER FALL
SO JUST CALL ME

AND YOU'LL SEE
THAT IM ALWAYS HERE
FOR YOU SO NEVER FEAR
IM ALWAYS NEAR
JUST LIKE EAGLES AND FRIENDSHIP

Goodbye

DATE: 11 26 96

WHY IS IT SO HARD TO SAY GOODBYE
I LOVE YOU
YOU NEVER LIED
SAYING GOODBYE HAS MADE ME BLUE
WHY DO WE HAVE TO SAY GOODBYE
WHEN IT MAKES ME BLUE
ALL IT DOES IS MAKE US CRY
WHAT SHOULD WE DO
GOODBYE WHY IS IT SO HARD
I MISS YOU
I KNOW YOU HOLD THE CARD
I KNOW YOU MISS ME TOO
WHAT IS IT TO SAY
WHEN ALL I LOVE
GOES WITH THE DAY
MAKES ME WANT A DOVE
WHAT IS TO DO
WHEN ALL I WANT IS GONE
EVERYTHING IN MY HEART IS BLUE
MAKES IT SEEM SO LONG
YOU WERE IN MY LIFE
YOU LEFT ME FOR SOMETHING NEW
YOU MAKE A GOOD LIFE
IT'S LIKE YOU GREW WINGS AND FLEW
WHEN YOU SAID GOODBYE
YOU CUT MY HEART LIKE A KNIFE
YOU WEREN'T EVEN SHY
BUT YOU'RE STILL IN MY LIFE
IT WASN'T SUCH A GOODBYE
FOR NOW IT WAS JUST BYE.

By My Side

DATE: 2 28 00

YOU ALWAYS STOOD BY MY SIDE
I COULD NEVER HIDE
I COULD ALWAYS CONFIDE IN YOU
THAT'S WHAT ILL ALWAYS DO
I WILL ALWAYS BE TRUE
I WILL NEVER BE BLUE
YOU'RE ALWAYS APART OF ME
THAT'S WHAT I BELIEVE
THIS IS HOW I FEEL
ILLUSIONS THAT CHANGE INTO SOMETHING REAL
I SEE THINGS LEFT MY EYES
THROUGH THAT OF THE SKYS
THINGS THAT I CAN'T DISGUISE
EVERYTHING THAT WILL BE
THROUGH MEMORIES THAT I SEE
I COULD NEVER HIDE
MY FEELINGS THAT WILL NEVER SUBSIDE
I KNOW YOU WILL ALWAYS BE BY MY SIDE
WHEN EVER I FALL
ALL I HAVE TO DO IS CALL
WHEN IM DOWN
YOU ALWAYS TURN THINGS AROUND
LIFT ME OFF THE GROUND
MAKE ME HAVE A BEAUTIFUL DAY
I WILL ALWAYS STAY
BY YOUR SIDE
SO DON'T EVER HIDE
ILL ALWAYS BE AROUND

TO LIFT YOU OFF THE GROUND
YOU HAVE MY HEART
THAT'S THE BEST PART
I KNOW IF I EVER SHED A TEAR
YOU WILL ALWAYS BE NEAR
I WILL NEVER FEAR
BECAUSE I HAVE YOU MY DEAR
I KNOW THAT YOU WILL ALWAYS REMAIN BY MY SIDE.

Love

DATE: 11 15 00

I NEVER THOUGHT I WOULD FIND YOU
BUT I HAVE IT FEELS SO TRUE
NOW I DON'T HAVE TO IMAGINE
A LOVE THAT DOESN'T EXIST
BECAUSE NOW I HAVE SOMETHING GENUINE
I REMEMBER THE FIRST TIME WE KISSED
NOW I DON'T HAVE TO WISH OF LOVE
WHEN SOME HOW IT WAS SENT FROM ABOVE
ALL OF WHAT I FEEL IS SO REAL
I DON'T HAVE TO IMAGINE A LOVE SO GENUINE
I CAN FEEL YOU
I KNOW IT HAS TO BE TRUE
IT'S SO STRONG
THAT IT DOESN'T FEEL WRONG
I FEEL YOU KISSING ME
I FEEL YOU LOVING ME
CARING FOR ME
I NEVER THOUGHT THIS COULD BE
NOW MY LOVE RUNS FREE
FOR YOU HAVE BRIGHTENED MY LIFE
NOW I DON'T HAVE A KNIFE
IN MY BACK
BECAUSE YOU DON'T LACK
I NEVER THOUGHT I WOULD BELIEVE
IN LOVE AGAIN
THEN AGAIN I WAS NEVER LOVED
BY SOMEONE LIKE YOU
SOMEONE I CAN KEEP TO THE END
ONE THAT WILL NEVER LEAVE
ONE SO TRUE
THAT NOW MY ONE AND ONLY
TRUE LOVE.

Will I Ever Be With You Again

DATE: 2 / 0 99

WILL I EVER BE WITH YOU AGAIN
MY FRIEND
MORE THEN FRIENDS AGAIN
ONCE THIS HEART OF MINE MENDS
WITH EVERYTHING IM ALONE
TO EVERYTHING THAT'S NOW UNKNOWN
NOW I'VE FALLEN
WITHOUT NOBODY CALLEN
I HOLD OUT MY HAND
FOR SOMEONE TO LIFT ME OUT OF THE SAND
NOW IM IN A DESERT LAND
I HAVE NO STRENGTH
WILL I EVER BE ABLE TO GO THE LENGTH
YOU'RE NOW MY FRIEND
ONCE AGAIN
WILL I EVER BE WITH YOU AGAIN
MORE THAN FRIENDS
ONCE AGAIN
THAT IS ALSO UNKNOWN
WITH THIS HEART THAT IS SO ALONE
I DON'T KNOW WHY
ILL STILL TRY
EVEN IF I CRY
NOW THAT WERE ONLY FRIENDS
ONCE AGAIN
UNKNOWING IF ILL EVER BE WITH YOU AGAIN
MORE THEN JUST FRIENDS
WITH A HEART THAT STILL HAS TO MEND

MAYBE SOMEDAY
WILL FIND A WAY
WITH THE RIGHT WORDS TO SAY
WILL GET BACK TOGETHER AGAIN
MORE THEN FRIENDS
MAYBE THIS TIME TO THE END
MY ONLY FRIEND
ILL FIND THE STRENGTH
TO GO THE EXTRA LENGTH
ILL PICK MY SELF UP
WILL BE TOUGH
OUT OF THIS LONELY LAND
TO LIFT MYSELF OUT OF THE SAND
WITHOUT A HAND
BUT WERE FRIENDS
ONCE AGAIN
MAYBE TO BE MORE THEN FRIENDS
ONCE AGAIN
AFTER OUR HEARTS MEND
MY FRIEND
MAYBE SOMEDAY
WILL FIND AWAY
WITH THE RIGHT WORDS TO SAY
WE CAN BE MORE THEN FRIENDS
ONCE AGAIN
MY FRIEND
WILL I EVER BE WITH YOU AGAIN?

Wild Love

DATE: 12 7 93

WILD LOVE
WILD ROSES
WILD FIRE
WILD HORSES
WHEN IM WITH YOU I WILL ALWAYS FEEL WILD LOVE
I SEE THAT OUR LOVE HAS FALLEN
WE MAY HAVE WILD ROSES BUT NOTHING COMPARES
TO WILD LOVE IN YOUR ARMS
WILD LOVE
WILD HORSES
WHEN IM WITH YOU I ALWAYS CARE ABOUT OUR WILD LOVE
I THINK THAT OUR LOVE IS WILD
IT COULD NEVER BE MILD
FOR IT RIDES ON WILD HORSES
NEVER KNOWING FOR SURE WHEN IT WILL SPIN
OR WHEN IT JUST MIGHT BUCK YOU OFF
THAT'S WHAT HAPPENS WHEN YOU HAVE WILD LOVE
RIDING ON WILD HORSES
BUT YOU ALWAYS HAVE IT IN YOUR MIND
WILL IT SPIN OR BUCK ME OFF THIS WILD RIDE
ON A PATCH OF WILD ROSES
OR WILD FIRE
WHILE OUR LOVE TAKES THIS WILD RIDE
LIKE WERE ON THE SPIN CYCLE
OUR WE HEADED FOR RINSE
ON WILD HORSES
SPINNING OUR WILD HEARTS
OR OUR WE GOING TO GET TURNED OFF

BEFORE WE GET BUCKED OFF
WILD HORSES
WILD FIRE
WILD ROSES
WILD LOVE.

Winter Is What I Feel

DATE: 10 15 98

FOR WHAT I FEEL
IT'S WINTER
I FEEL IT IN THE MIDDLE OF THE DAY
SO ILL STAY WITH WHAT I SAY
THAT IS SO REAL
THIS FEELS LIKE A SPLINTER
I DON'T KNOW WHAT TO DO
BUT FEEL THESE COLD NIGHTS
THAT HAVE NO LIGHT
BUT WHAT I SEE
IS THE STARS UP ABOVE
THAT ARE SO BRIGHT
THAT I DON'T NEED A LIGHT
FOR THESE COLD NIGHTS
I CANT BELIEVE
THAT I CANT LEAVE
BUT WITH THIS RHYME
THAT'S SUSPENDED IN TIME
BECAUSE OF THIS FRIGHT
ON THESE COLD DARK NIGHTS
OF NOT HAVING ANY SIGHT
WITHOUT THE STARS THAT SHINE SO BRIGHT
THAT GIVE OFF SUCH LIGHT
THAT I MIGHT
NEVER SEE
WHAT I HAVE IN ME
THAT ONE OF THESE NIGHTS AND DAYS
THAT NEEDS TO BE SET FREE
FOR I LOST THE KEY
TO IT ALL
WHEN MY HEART TOOK A GREAT FALL
IN THE WINTER

THAT SOMETIMES I DON'T KNOW WHY BUT IT FEELS LIKE A SPLINTER
FROM A HEART
THAT FELL APART
NOW IT'S WINTER
THAT'S WHY EVERYTHING FEELS LIKE A SPLINTER
WINTER.

You

HAVING YOU NEXT TO ME
WAS A SIGHT TO SEE
EVEN ON THE SCARIEST OF NIGHTS
YOU EYES GIVE SUCH LIGHT
MEMORIES THAT I HOPE YOU NEVER REGRET
I DON'T KNOW HOW I EVER SAID GOODBYE
WITH TEARS IN MY EYES
HAVING YOU BY MY SIDE
KNOWING I DIDN'T HAVE TO HIDE
FROM THE PAIN
THAT STILL REMAINED
THE PAIN I TRIED TO REFRAIN
HAVING YOU HOLD ME TIGHT
HAD FELT SO RIGHT
I WISH I HAD KNOWN WHAT TO SAY
ON THAT DAY
NOW ALL I KNOW
IS THAT YOU'LL BE IN MY HEART
FROM THIS DAY ON
AND FOREVER
YOU

WHAT TO DO
I GET QUESTIONED ABOUT YOU
I DON'T KNOW WHAT TO SAY
SO I TAKE IT DAY BY BAY
WHAT TO DO
I CANT DENY THAT I LOVE YOU
I TRY TO KEEP FRIENDS
SO ILL TRY TO MAKE A MENDS
ALL I KNOW IS THAT
ILL DEFEND YOU
ILL ALWAYS BE TRUE
WHAT TO DO
I THINK ABOUT YOU
I DON'T KNOW WHAT TO DO
ILL TRY TO FIGURE IT OUT
WHAT IT IS ALL ABOUT
YOU HAVE A GIRLFRIEND
THAT ILL DEFEND
I GOT FEELINGS FOR YOU
I DON'T KNOW WHAT TO DO

DATE: 7 9 97

WHERE THERE IS LOVE, THE HEART IS LIGHT
WHERE THERE IS LOVE, THE DAY IS BRIGHT
WHERE THERE IS LOVE, THERE IS A SONG
TO HELP WHEN THINGS ARE GOING WRONG
WHERE THERE IS LOVE, THERE IS A SMILE
TO HELP WHEN THINGS SEEM MORE WORTHWHILE
WHERE THERE IS LOVE, THERE IS QUIET PEACE
A TRANQUIL PLACE TURMOILS CEASE
LOVE CHANGES DARKNESS INTO LIGHT
MAKES THE HEART TAKES WINGLESS FLIGHT
OH, BLESSED ARE THEY WHO WALK IN LOVE
WHO ALSO WALK WITH GOD UP ABOVE,
WHEN MEN WALK WITH GOD AGAIN
THERE SHALL BE QUIET PEACE ON EARTH FOR ALL.

What I Know

DATE: 7 9 05

I KNOW THAT I LOVE YOU
YOU'RE SO TRUE
YOU'RE ALWAYS SO KIND
I KNOW THAT I CARE ABOUT YOU
ALL THE TIME
BUT THIS IS WHAT I WANT TO DO
I KNOW THIS PROBABLY DON'T RHYME
I KNOW THAT YOU'RE IN MY HEART
YOU'RE IN MY LIFE
WE'VE GROWN APART
YOU'RE THE REASON TO SURVIVE
I KNOW THAT YOU'RE MY STRENGTH
I HAD FALLEN
YOU SAID I COULD GO THE LENGTH
I'VE BEEN STALLEN
I KNOW MY HEART BREAKS
THAT'S FINE
ILL DO WHAT IT TAKES
TO MAKE YOU MINE
I KNOW I WAS GETTING OVER HIM
WHEN I MET YOU
MY LIFE DIDN'T SEEM SO DIM
NOW I WAS LEFT BLUE
I KNOW I SAW WHERE IT ALL BEGINS
I KNOW AS I SEE WHERE IT ALL ENDS
IT'S LEAVING ME BLUE ALL OVER AGAIN
I LOVE YOU THAT'S WHAT I KNOW.

What I Want To Say

DATE: 12 7 93

I DON'T WANT TO SAY
HOW MUCH I LOVE YOU
BECAUSE I DON'T WANT TO LOSE YOU
I DON'T WANT TO SAY
HOW I FEEL ABOUT YOU
I DON'T WANT TO FIND A NEW MARE
I DON'T WANT TO SAY
HOW MUCH YOU MEAN TO ME
I DON'T WANT TO LEAN ON SOME ONE ELSE
I DON'T WANT TO SAY
HOW MUCH I FEAR FOR YOU
I DON'T WANT TO END UP IN TEARS FOR YOU
I DON'T WANT TO SAY
HOW MUCH I CARE FOR YOU
I DON'T WANT TO SCARE YOU
I DON'T WANT TO SAY
HOW MUCH I NEED YOU
I DON'T WANT TO FIND A NEW SEED
I DON'T WANT TO SAY
HOW MUCH I WANT TO SEE YOU EACH DAY
BECAUSE I DON'T WANT YOU TO PUSH ME AWAY
I DON'T WANT TO SAY
HOW MUCH I THINK OF YOU
BECAUSE I DON'T WANT YOU TO SINK
I DON'T WANT TO SAY MUCH OF ANYTHING
BECAUSE I LOVE YOU TO MUCH.

We Can Last Forever

DATE: 12 11 94

WE CAN LAST FOREVER
BECAUSE WE ARE FRIENDS
FOREVER SO WE CAN STAY TOGETHER
WE HAVE BEEN THROUGH
THICK AND THIN BUT THAT'S
WHY WE ARE FRIENDS FOREVER
WE CAN STAY TOGETHER
CAUSE WE ARE FRIENDS FOREVER
WE WILL STAY TOGETHER FOREVER
BECAUSE WE CAN LAST FOREVER.

Walk

AS I WALK
I WALK ALONE
WHILE I WALK
I MEET SOMEONE
AS WE WALK
WE WALK ALONE
WHILE WE WALK
WE MEET SOMEONE ELSE
THEN WE ALL WALK
TOGETHER AS ONE
IF YOU WANT TO BE MY FRIEND
THEN WALK BESIDE ME
NOT AGAINST ME
NOT BEHIND ME
OR IN FRONT OF ME
WALK BESIDE ME
AND WALK AS MY FRIEND
NOW WE WALK AS FRIENDS
ALL TOGETHER AS ONE.

VALENTINES DAY
I WAS HOPING TO FIND SOMEWAY
MAYBE EVEN SOMEDAY
TO BE WITH YOU AGAIN ON THIS DAY
I GUESS ILL NEVER SEE
WHAT USED TO BE
AGAIN
I GUESS WHAT ILL SEE IS US ALWAYS BEING FRIENDS
TO THE END
NEVER TO BE YOUR GIRLFRIEND AGAIN
I SUPPOSE IT'S OVER TO THE END
SO MUCH FOR TIME TO MEND
LOOKS LIKE I LOST YOU
NOW WHAT DO I DO
WITH THIS LOVE I HAVE FOR YOU
SO MUCH FOR HEARING THAT YOU LOVE ME TOO
ALONE
ON THIS DAY
THAT I THOUGHT I WOULD SEE SOMEDAY
IN SOMEWAY
VALENTINES DAY
ALONE
TO EVERYTHING THAT I'VE KNOWN
EVERYTHING I'VE SHOWN
BECAUSE I'VE BLOWN
EVERYTHING THAT I'VE ONCE KNOWN
WITH YOU
BUT I LOVE YOU
I WAS HOPING TO BE WITH YOU AGAIN

MORE THEN FRIENDS
BUT IM TO BE ALONE
NEVER TO SEE WHAT I'VE KNOWN AGAIN
VALENTINES DAY
FOR SWEETHEARTS
THAT I THOUGHT WOULD BE ANOTHER START
FOR US AGAIN
TO BECOME MORE THEN FRIENDS
TO HEAR YOU SAY YOU LOVE ME TOO
WHEN I GOT BACK WITH YOU
IM TRYING SO HARD TO BE TRUE
NOW IM BLUE
ONCE AGAIN
STILL ONLY TO BE FRIENDS
SOMEDAY
SOMEWAY
WE'LL BE TOGETHER AGAIN ON THIS DAY
VALENTINES DAY!
VALENTINES DAY!

Walking Through The Night

DATE: 3 5 00

AS I WALK THROUGH THE NIGHT
ALL ALONE
WITH VERY LITTLE LIGHT
FEELING SO UNKNOWN
THINKING OF WHAT WE HAD
THAT MADE ME GLAD
LOOKING UP AT THE MOON
HOPING TO SEE YOU SOON
AS I KEEP ON GOING
WITHOUT KNOWING
WHATS AHEAD OF ME
AND WHAT I SEE
YOULL NEVER BELIEVE
AN ANGEL WATCHING OVER ME
AT THAT MOMENT I FELT FREE
AS I WALK THROUGH THE NIGHT
WITH VERY LITTLE LIGHT
I WASN'T ALONE
I STILL FELT UNKNOWN
THE ANGEL HAD SHOWN ME
EVEN THOUGH I COULD BEARLY SEE
THINGS AHEAD OF ME
NOT TO BE FRIGHTENED
THAT THINGS WILL BRIGHTEN
ON DOWN THE ROAD
SO NO MATTER HOW DARK THE NIGHT
I WILL NEVER BE ALONE.

Unknown

DATE: 3 6 00

EVERYTHING FEELS SO UNKNOWN
IN A LIFE THAT'S SO ALONE
WHAT DO I DO NOW
WHEN I DON'T HAVE YOU
EVERYTHING FEELS SO NEW
I DON'T KNOW HOW TO GO ON
WHEN EVERYTHING IS GONE
YOU ALWAYS WERE THERE
THINGS WE USED TO SHARE
THAT FEELING WITH YOU WAS SO RARE
NOW I DON'T HAVE IT
NOW THOSE FEELINGS DON'T FIT
WITH THIS LONELY LIFE
WHEN IT FEELS LIKE A KNIFE
HOW CAN I FIND THAT FEELING AGAIN
THAT I SHARED WITH YOU
WHEN I FOUND IT IN A FRIEND
WHAT DO I DO
WHEN EVERYTHING FEELS SO NEW
SO UNKNOWN
AND I FEEL SO ALONE.

Trying

DATE: 4 / 7 96

TRYING TO LOSE MY PARANOIA
IT'S SO HARD
I DON'T KNOW WHAT TO DO
EXCEPT TO CRY
IT'S LIKE A CARD
THAT YOU SEEM TO LOSE
I DON'T KNOW WHY
I DON'T WANT TO LOSE YOU
SO I'VE GOT TO LOSE THE OBSESSION
BECAUSE I LOVE YOU
I KNOW IT HURTS
YOU MEAN SO MUCH
SO I KNOW WHAT I GOTTA DO
BEFORE THIS TAKES POSSESSION
BECAUSE I KNOW MY FEELINGS ARE TRUE
THIS IS NO CERTS
ITS JUST THAT I WANT YOUR TOUCH
TRYING TO KEEP YOU
ITS NOT EASY
BUT LOSING YOU IS EVEN HARDER
BECAUSE YOU'RE MY LIFE
BUT I WANT YOU THIS IS TRUE
IM NOT CRAZY
BUT I SCREAM LOUDER.

The Song Of Love

DATE: 4 9 96

IF THERE WAS A SONG I KNEW
I COULD SING IT TO YOU
I WOULD SING THE SONG OF LOVE
IF THERE WAS WORDS TO EXPRESS HOW I FEEL ABOUT YOU
I WOULD SING THE SONG OF LOVE
IF THERE WAS A WAY I COULD TELL
YOU HOW MUCH YOU MEAN
THE WORLD TO ME
I COULD SING THE SONG OF LOVE
IF THERE WAS A WAY I COULD TELL
YOU HOW MUCH I LOVE YOU
I SING A SONG, THE SONG OF LOVE
IF THERE WAS ANYTHING I COULD
DO TO EXPRESS HOW I FEEL
IT WOULD BE IN THE SONG OF LOVE
THERE IS SO MUCH I WANT TO TELL YOU
THAT I COULD SING A SONG OR WRITE A POEM
TO SING TO YOU ON HOW I FEEL
IT WOULD HAVE TO BE A SONG, THE SONG OF LOVE
IF THERE WAS A WAY TO TELL YOU ALL I WANT IS YOU
I WOULD SING YOU THE SONG OF LOVE
TO TELL YOU EVERYTHING I WANT TO TELL YOU.
THE SONG OF LOVE!

Strong Love

DATE: 4 9 96

WHAT IS LOVE
I WISH I KNEW
I THINK IT'S A DOVE
I BELIEVE ITS YOU
IT COULD BE RIGHT
IT COULD BE WRONG
BUT I BELIEVE ITS STRONG
IT COULD HURT
IT COULD MAKE YOU HAPPY
IT WILL MAKE YOU SEARCH
IT'S A NEW LOVE
A TRUE LOVE
MOSTLY IT'S A STRONG LOVE
IT COULD BE LONG
IT COULD BE SHORT
I BELIEVE IT'S A SONG
IT'S HARD TO SORT
OUT BUT TRUE LOVE
IS SOMETHING TO BE APART OF
IT IS A STRONG LOVE.

WHY I LOVE
THIS DOVE
BECAUSE IM
SO TRUE
WHY DO I WANT TO BE
SO BLUE
WHEN I CAN THINK
OF YOU
WHY DO I CARE FOR
THIS MARE
WHY DO I FLY WHEN I
CAN TRY
WHY DO I RUN FAST WHEN WE
CAN LAST
WHY DO WE FIGHT WHEN WE
CAN SIGHT
WHY ARE WE SO MEAN WHEN WE
CAN LEAN
WHY DO YOU LOOK
WHEN YOU TOOK
BECAUSE I LOVE
THIS DOVE!

Poem 3

DATE: 12 7 93

I LOVE
THIS DOVE
I CARE
BUT FEAR
I THINK
HE SINKS
I CRY
HE TRIES
I FLY
HE TIES
I LIVE
HE LIVES
I CRY
I FIGHT
HE SIGHTS
I HURT
HE FLIRTS
POEM
POEM.

Printed in the United States
by Baker & Taylor Publisher Services